THE 5 NUTRIENT CYCLES

SCIENCE BOOK 3RD GRADE
CHILDREN'S SCIENCE EDUCATION BOOKS

BABY PROFESSOR
EDUCATION KIDS

Speedy Publishing LLC
40 E. Main St. #1156
Newark, DE 19711
www.speedypublishing.com

In this book, we're going to talk about the 5 nutrient cycles. So, let's get right to it!

WHAT ARE NUTRIENTS?

A nutrient is a substance that an organism needs to stay alive and stay healthy. For example, human beings need oxygen to breathe. Without oxygen we can't stay alive.

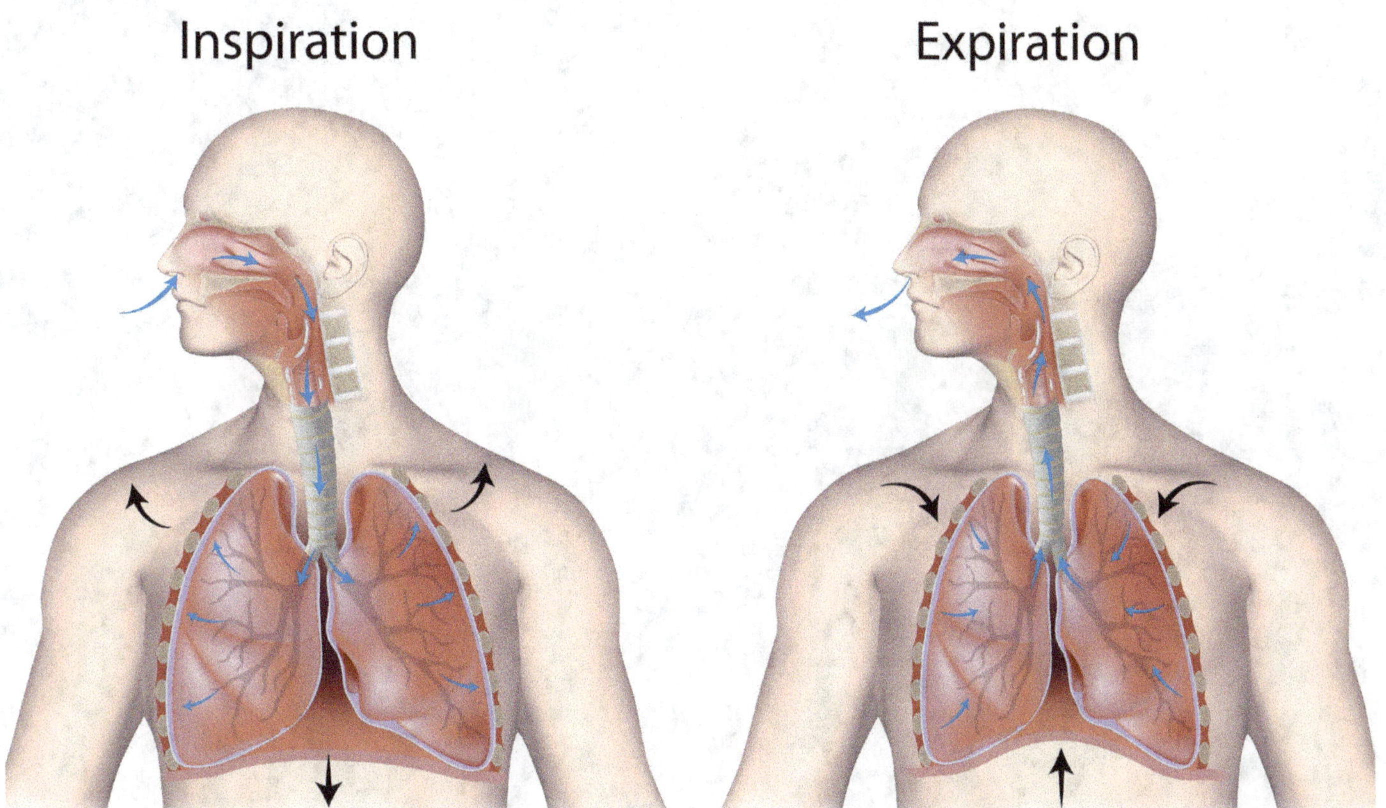
Inspiration
Expiration

There are some key elements on Earth that are necessary for all plants and animals to stay alive. These key elements are:

Carbon, chemical symbol C
Oxygen, chemical symbol O
Hydrogen, chemical symbol H
Nitrogen, chemical symbol N
Phosphorus, chemical symbol P

Each of these nutrients has a cycle. The cycle describes how the element is used by plants and animals, how it gets moved through living and nonliving things, and how it's recycled to be used again.

In order for this cycle to happen, the nutrient goes through three different types of processes:

- Biological, as in being eaten by animals or by absorption through plants and also through elimination of waste products

- Geological, as in the soil
- Chemical, as in chemical reactions

Because they go through all these different processes, nutrient cycles are called biogeochemical cycles.

IS THE CYCLE LOCAL OR IS IT GLOBAL?

There are two main types of biogeochemical cycles. They can be global or they can be local. For example, oxygen travels through the air. It can also travel through the soil or through water. Because the main way it travels is in the air, it may travel for a long distance before a person or animal breathes it in. This means that oxygen has a global cycle.

This is also true of the elements nitrogen, hydrogen, and carbon. Although they can be found in air, water, and soil, the atmosphere is the main way they travel for a long distance, so they are global cycles.

On the other hand, a nutrient such as phosphorus gets recycled through the soil. There are other important nutrients that get recycled through the soil too, such as calcium and potassium. If a nutrient gets recycled mainly through soil, then it has a local biogeochemical cycle.

Let's look at each cycle in detail.

CARBON CYCLE

All organisms on Earth are based on the element of carbon. In fact, sometimes human beings are described as "carbon-based" life forms. Carbon makes up about 18% of your body weight.

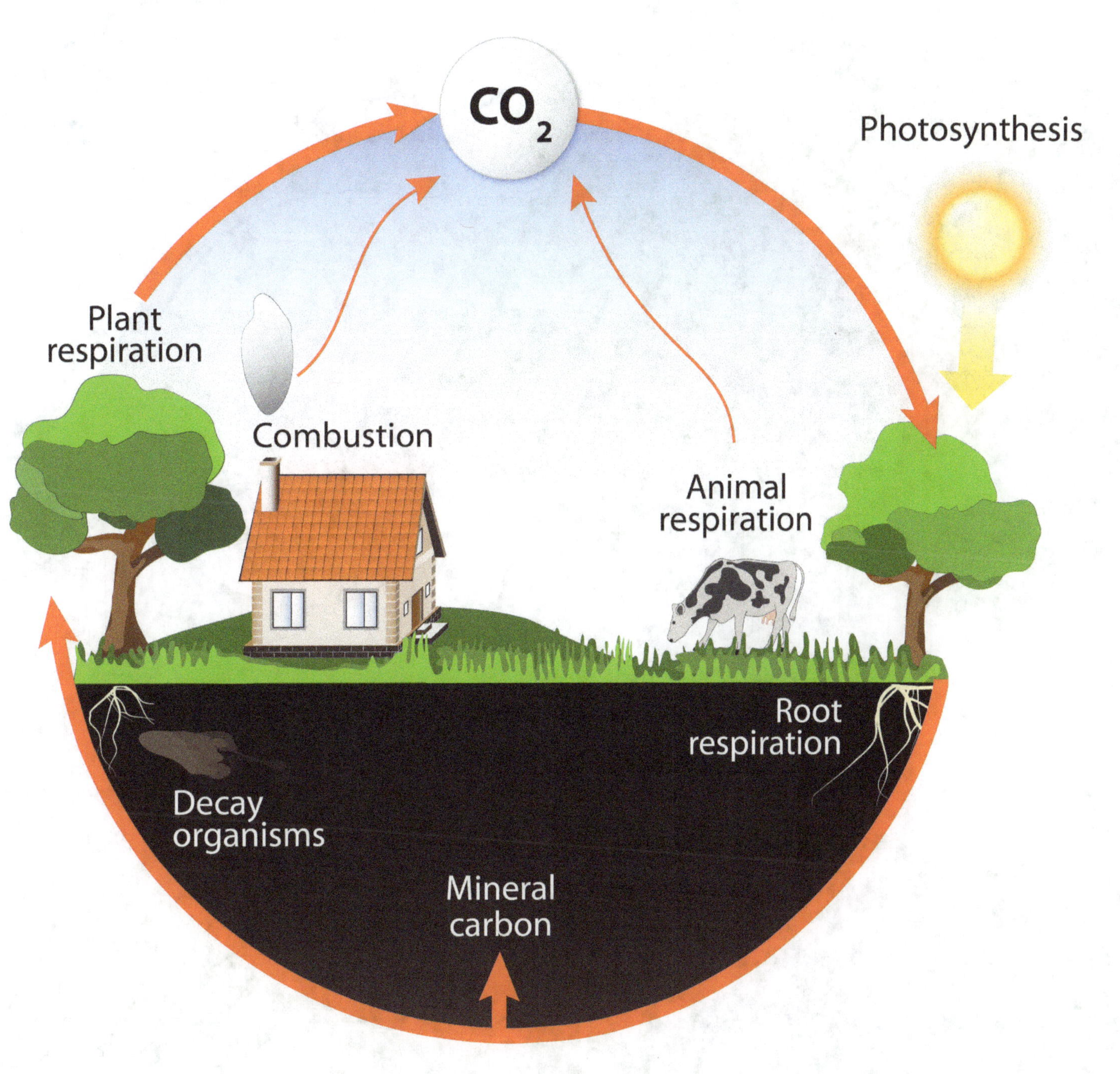
CO_2
Photosynthesis
Plant respiration
Combustion
Animal respiration
Root respiration
Decay organisms
Mineral carbon

O_2
CO_2

At any point in time some atoms of carbon are moving through air, water, or soil. The element of carbon is used during many different biogeochemical processes. The carbon cycle and the oxygen cycle are connected with each other.

CARBON COMES OUT OF THE ATMOSPHERE

Natural processes are always withdrawing the element of carbon from the atmosphere. This action of withdrawing carbon in the form of carbon dioxide or CO2 is described as a "carbon sink." Don't think of it as a kitchen sink. Think of it as a sinkhole! It's an environment where more carbon sinks in than comes out.

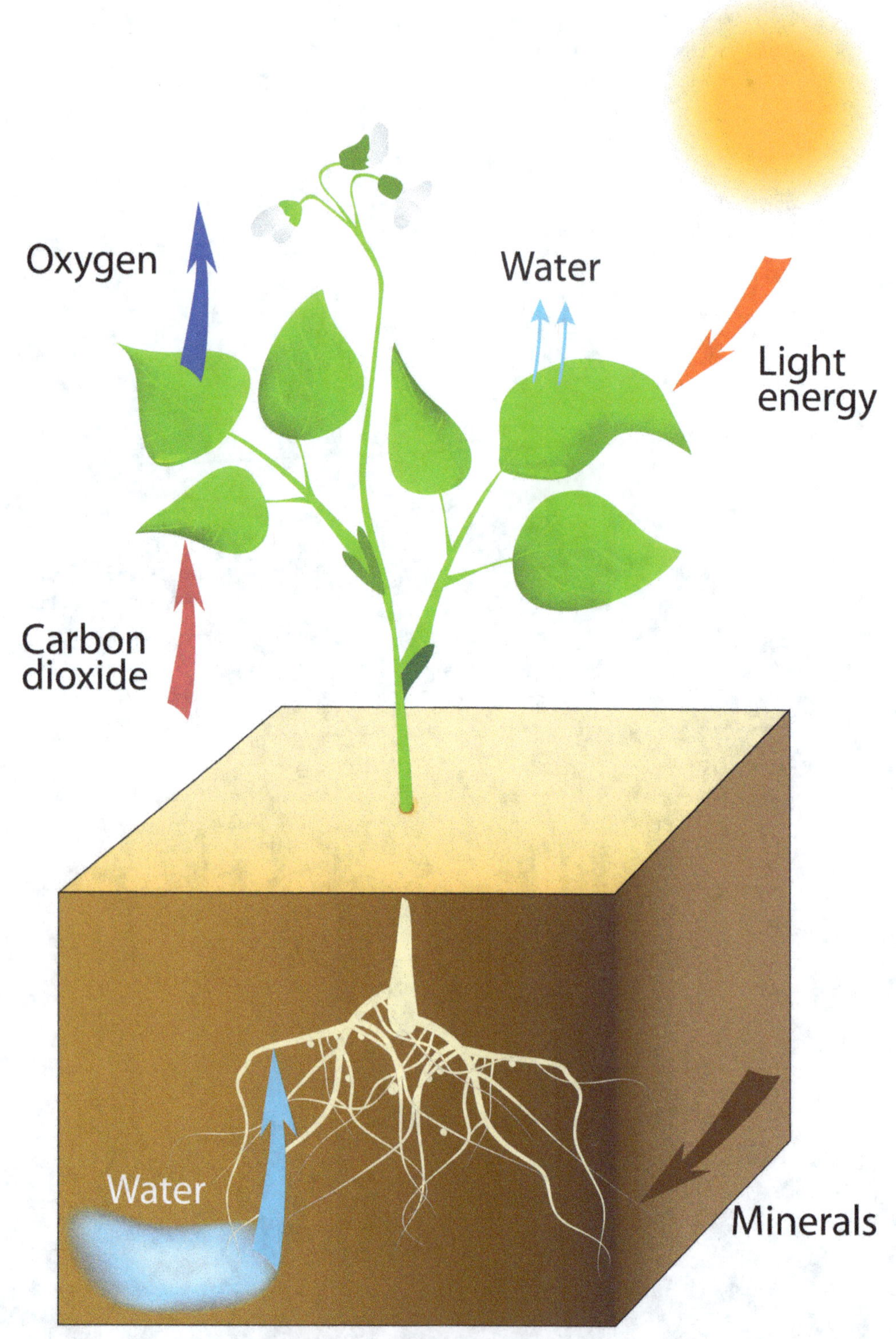
Oxygen
Water
Light energy
Carbon dioxide
Water
Minerals

Plants use carbon dioxide, energy from the sun, and water during the process of photosynthesis. They take CO2, sunlight, and H2O and transform it into oxygen as well as a form of sugar they can use for food. Large regions that have many types of plants like the Amazon rainforest withdraw lots of CO2 from the atmosphere. In other words, the Amazon rainforest has an enormous "carbon sink."

The saltwater in the oceans removes extra $CO2$ in the air as well. Carbon dioxide traveling in the air has a chemical reaction with the salty seawater. The end result of that reaction is a compound called carbonic acid. An excess of this compound isn't good, because it can cause acid rain, which is toxic to the environment. However, carbonic acid in small quantities is good. In fact, there are many sea creatures that use it to construct their shells. Eventually, when these creatures die, their shells go to the bottom of the ocean and become layers of sedimentary rock, such as limestone.

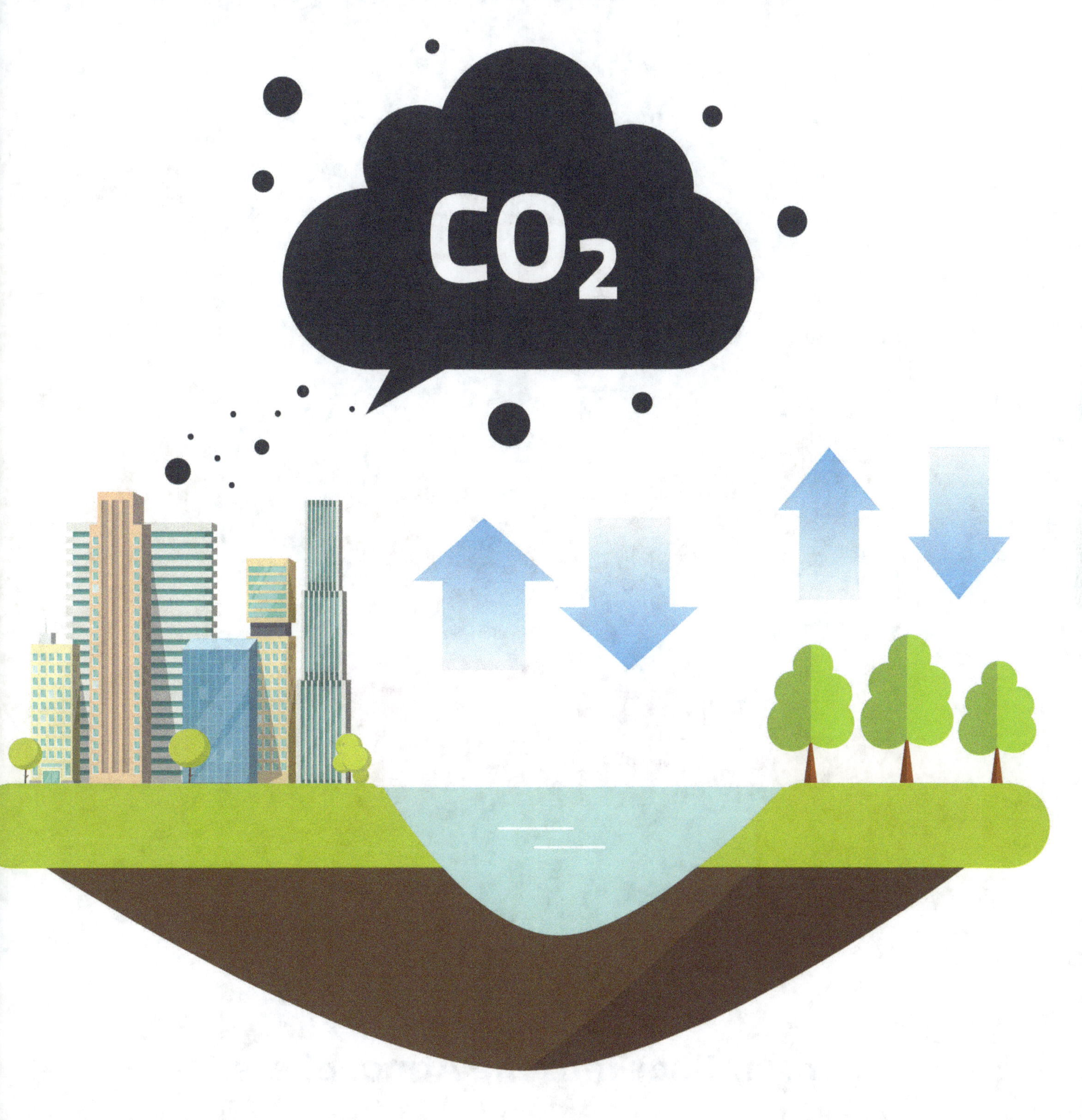
CO_2

Carbon Goes Into the Atmosphere...

The opposite of “sinks” is “sources.” As carbon sinks are occurring, other processes are putting carbon back into the atmosphere. All the animals on Earth including human beings breathe in oxygen and let out carbon dioxide as a waste product. This happens with every breath you take.

Another way that carbon gets back into the environment is when animals and plants die. Their bodies decay and then the carbon goes into the atmosphere or into the soil. Over many millions of years, that carbon turns into fossil fuels like oil.

When organic matter is burned, such as trees or shrubs or fossil fuels, then one of the chemicals released into the atmosphere is carbon.

THE CYCLE OF CARBON BALANCE

Nature does a wonderful job balancing the amount of carbon in the atmosphere. However, human populations have upset this balance by burning too many fossil fuels, such as coal and oil. If too much carbon goes into the atmosphere, then it can't be absorbed naturally by plants. Another destructive problem occurs when too many trees are cut down because it reduces the amount of carbon that can be converted into oxygen.

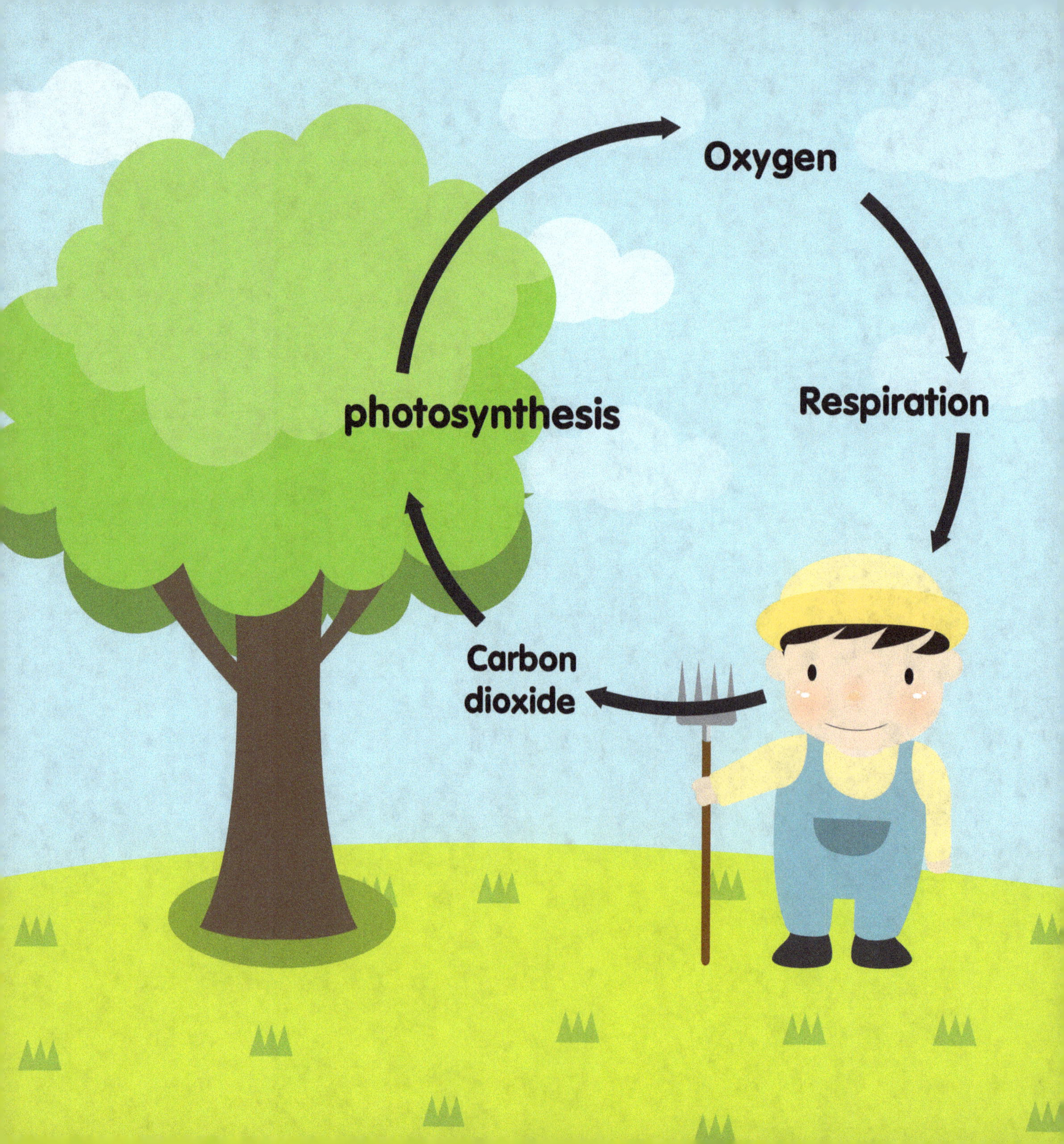
Oxygen
Respiration
photosynthesis
Carbon
dioxide

OXYGEN CYCLE

Over 65% of the human body is made up of oxygen and the main portion of that oxygen is a compound of hydrogen and oxygen, H2O, which is water. A very basic example of how the oxygen cycle works is the way we breathe and release carbon dioxide or CO2. All animals on Earth including humans breathe in oxygen and then release carbon dioxide. Plants absorb oxygen too. This process of taking in oxygen is called respiration. Through the process of photosynthesis, plants take in carbon dioxide and release oxygen. This completes the cycle, which starts all over again.

OXYGEN COMES OUT OF THE ATMOSPHERE

Respiration isn't the only way that oxygen is used up. Another way that oxygen is used is in the process of decomposition. When the bodies of plants and animals decompose after death, oxygen is used and carbon dioxide is emitted.

Have you ever seen old tools outdoors that have rusted? The process of oxidation uses up oxygen and the result is rust. Another thing that uses up oxygen is fire. When wood or other types of fuels burn they use up oxygen and release carbon dioxide.

OXYGEN GOES INTO THE ATMOSPHERE

Plants are critical because without them we wouldn't have oxygen. Most of the oxygen created on Earth comes from the plant process of photosynthesis. Some oxygen is also created from the reaction of sunlight and water in the atmosphere that is in the form of water vapor, which is essentially water suspended in air.

PRECIPITATION
CONDENSATION
RUN OFF
EVAPORATION
RIVER
OCEAN

HYDROGEN CYCLE

The hydrosphere is all the water on the surface of the Earth and also includes water that is above the surface of the Earth, such as clouds. Water has two hydrogen atoms for every one oxygen atom. Both plants and animals need water to survive. The hydrosphere gets hydrogen, its most plentiful element, from water. During the process of photosynthesis, water combines with carbon dioxide and forms glucose, a form of sugar. Hydrogen is produced as an end result of this process.

The compounds that hydrogen creates are important to the foods animals eat. Animals get both glucose and protein from eating plants. Hydrogen is a component of the carbohydrates we eat in foods that contain sugar and starch.

Hydrogen atom
(H)

The transmission of hydrogen atoms to water to the formation of carbohydrates and other compounds and then back to water through living organisms is a summary of how the hydrogen cycle works.

NITROGEN CYCLE

Nitrogen is critical to life on Earth. It's a necessary element of biological molecules such as nucleic and amino acids. There is a lot of nitrogen in the atmosphere but most organisms can't use this form of nitrogen. In order for nitrogen to be absorbed, it has to change into different forms. Bacteria take nitrogen from the atmosphere and change it into ammonia so it can be used.

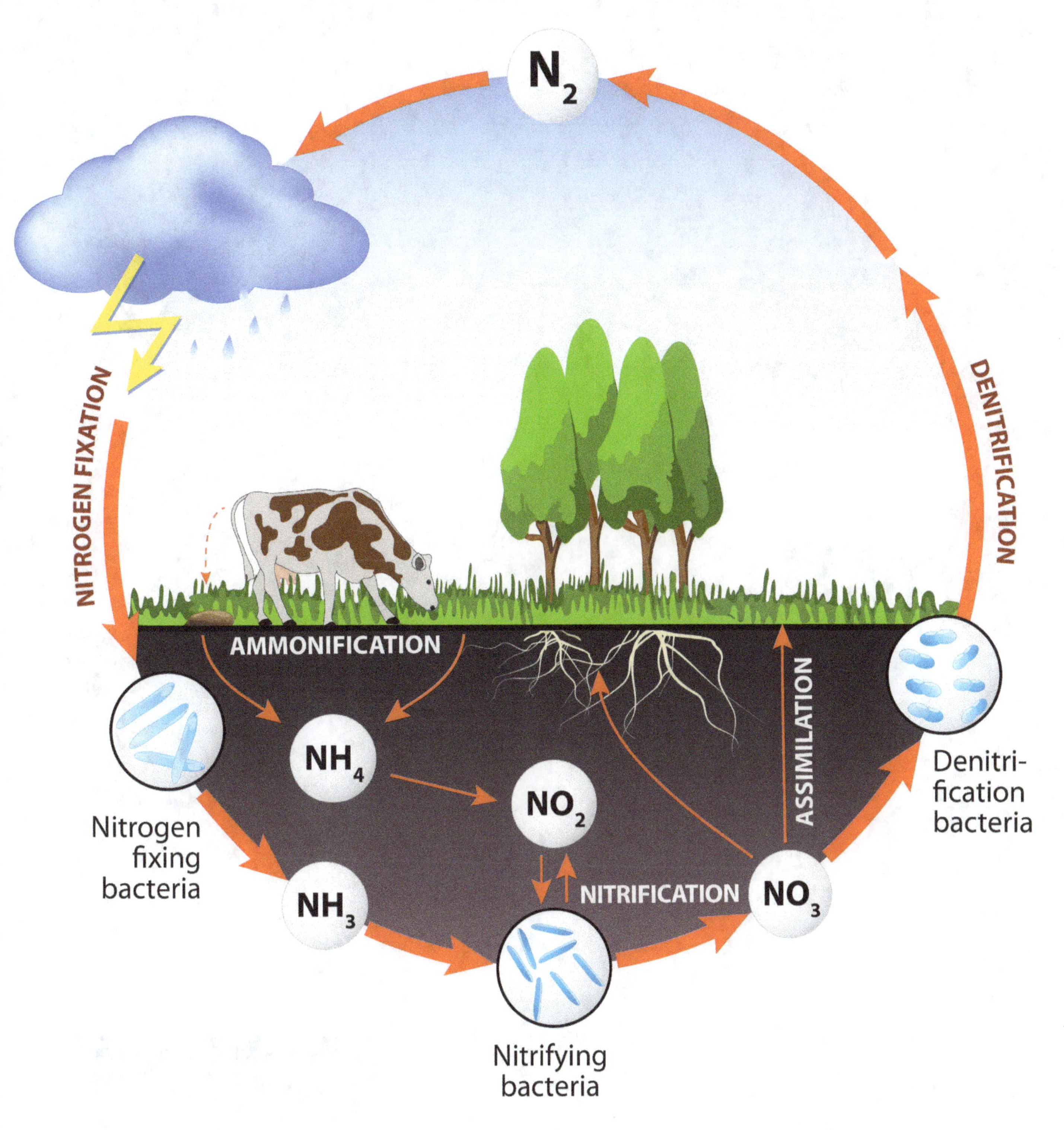

N_2
NITROGEN FIXATION
DENITRIFICATION
AMMONIFICATION
NH_4
NO_2
ASSIMILATION
Nitrogen fixing bacteria
Denitri-fication bacteria
NH_3
NITRIFICATION
NO_3
Nitrifying bacteria

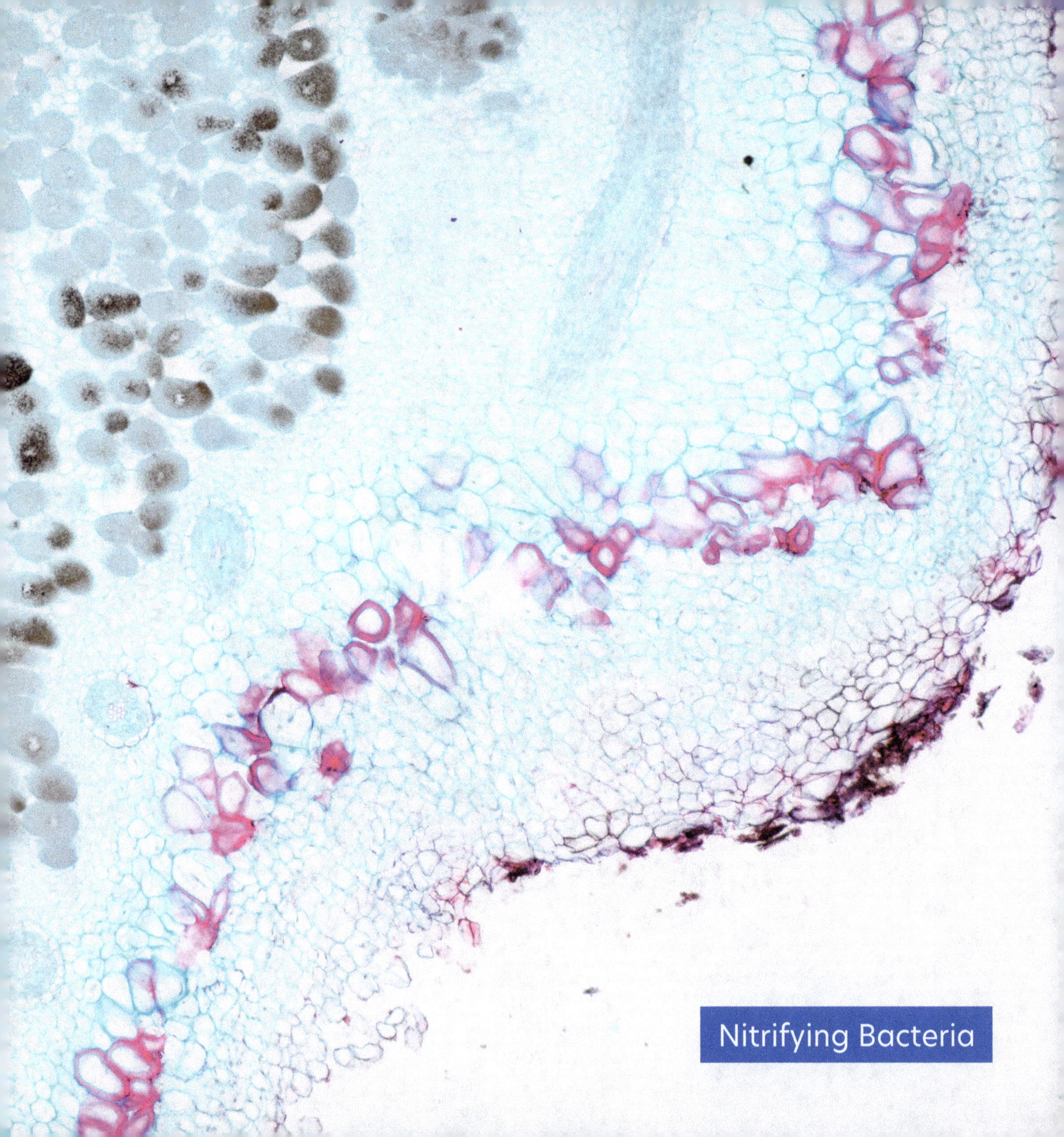
Nitrifying Bacteria

HERE IS HOW THE NITROGEN CYCLE WORKS:

Bacteria in water as well as in the soil change nitrogen in the air, which is N2, into NH3, which is ammonia.

Special types of bacteria called nitrifying bacteria change the ammonia or NH3 into two different forms—nitrite as well as nitrate.

Plants get nitrogen by absorbing a substance called ammonium (NH4+) by way of their roots. They also absorb nitrate this way. The plants create organic compounds using ammonium and nitrate.

Animals get nitrogen when they eat plants or other animals.

When animals or plants decay, the decomposers put ammonia (NH3) back into the ground.

Special bacteria known as nitrifying bacteria convert the ammonia to nitrate as well as nitrite.

Another type of bacteria, the denitrifying type, converts both nitrate and nitrite back to atmospheric nitrogen (N2) and it goes back into the atmosphere and completes the cycle.

PHOSPHORUS CYCLE

Remember that phosphorus is the only one of these five nutrients that is mostly circulated through the soil as well as through living organisms and water. This process makes its cycle local instead of global. Erosion of rocks containing phosphorus is what ensures that this nutrient gets into the soil. It's absorbed by plants and then those plants are consumed by animals. Once the animals die and are decomposed, the phosphorus returns to the soil.

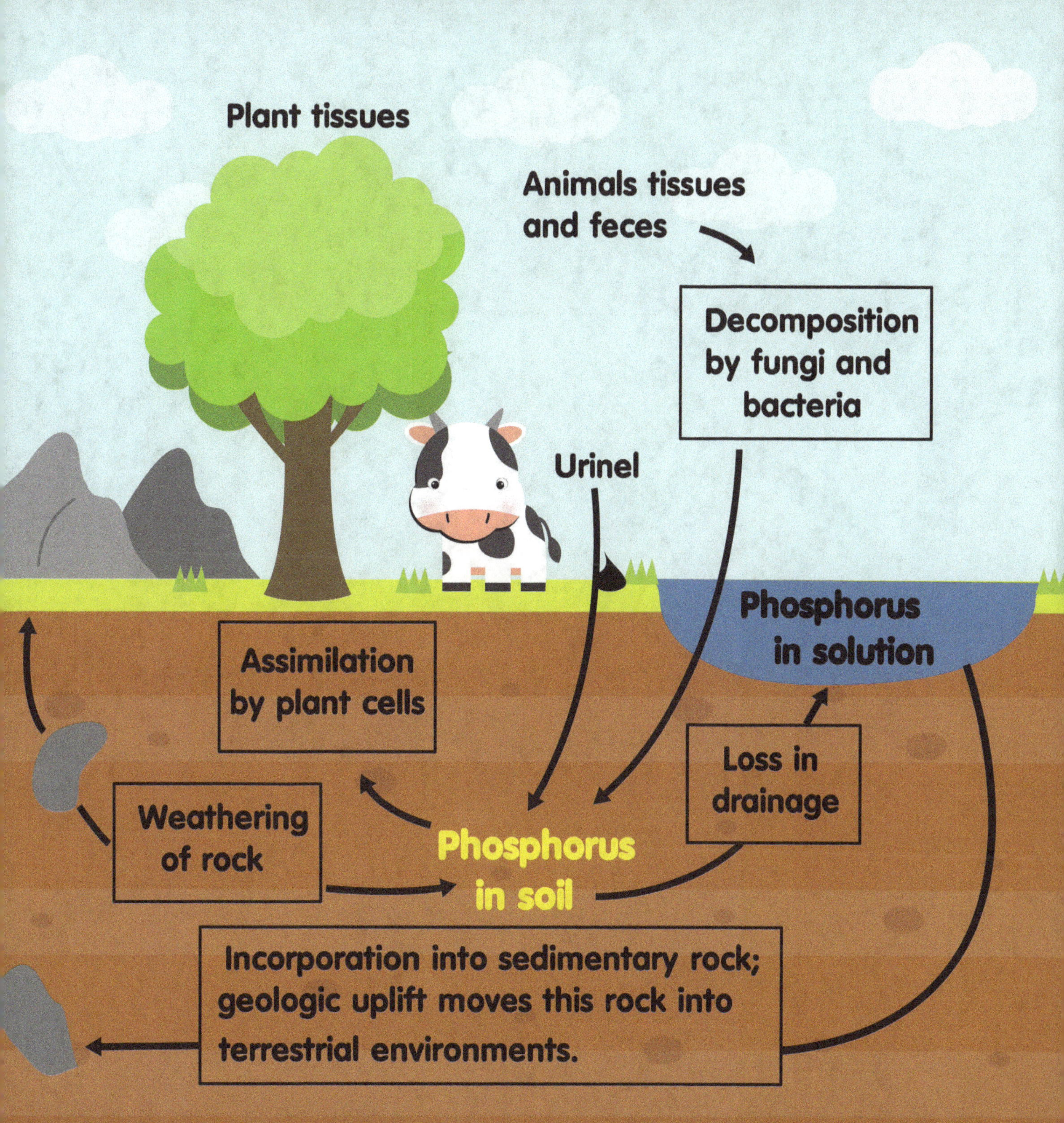
Plant tissues
Animals tissues and feces
Decomposition by fungi and bacteria
Urinel
Phosphorus in solution
Assimilation by plant cells
Loss in drainage
Weathering of rock
Phosphorus in soil
Incorporation into sedimentary rock; geologic uplift moves this rock into terrestrial environments.

SUMMARY

There are many nutrients that are important to the life and health of animals and plants. Oxygen and carbon are critical. Hydrogen, nitrogen, and phosphorus are also vital. Each of these five nutrients has a cycle where it is absorbed by animals and plants and then replaced into the atmosphere, water, and soil where it is recycled for use again.

Awesome! Now that you've read about the 5 nutrient cycles, you may want to read more information about decomposers that are important to the nutrient cycles in the Baby Professor book Fungi Are Not Plants - Biology Book Grade 4.

www.ingramcontent.com/pod-product-compliance
Lightning Source LLC
LaVergne TN
LVHW060507170826
845677LV00026B/1640

* 9 7 9 8 8 6 9 4 3 4 9 3 7 *